Sky Pony Press books may be purchased in bulk at special discounts for sales promotion, corporate gifts, fund-raising, or educational purposes. Special editions can also be created to specifications. For details, contact the Special Sales Department, Sky Pony Press, 307 West 36th Street, 11th Floor, New York, NY 10018 or info@skyhorsepublishing.com.

Sky Pony® is a registered trademark of Skyhorse Publishing, Inc.®, a Delaware corporation.

Visit our website at www.skyponypress.com.

10 9 8 7 6 5 4 3 2 1

Manufactured in China, February 2024
This product conforms to CPSIA 2008

Library of Congress Cataloging-in-Publication Data is available on file.

Cover design by Ramona Karl & Kai Texel
Cover illustrations by Nikolai Renger
US Edition edited by Nicole Frail

Print ISBN: 978-1-5107-7709-5
Ebook ISBN: 978-1-5107-7710-1

Using the Internet for Virtual School

Rules and Tips for a Successful Online Learning Experience

Written by Dagmar Geisler
Illustrated by Nikolai Renger
Translated by Andy Jones Berasaluce

Sky Pony Press
New York

Table of Contents

Best Friends

Madison is on her way to Luke's. The two have been friends for a very long time. Madison can't even remember how it started. In the sandbox? Maybe the day Madison got her new excavator toy and Luke wanted to play with it, too?

Regardless, it's nice to have a best friend like that in class.

Madison also likes Luke's big brother, Tim. He's nice and always so funny. Hopefully he's there today, too. He might even help her with her difficult math homework. It's really tricky. Usually, Madison figures out everything easily but not this time.

Luke has revealed to her that Tim has recently fallen in love.
Her name is Aileen, and she's in his class.

Madison knows her from gymnastics. She can understand why
Tim's in love with her. Aileen is incredibly good at
gymnastics, and she's also friendly and pretty.

Madison sighs. Maybe she's a little jealous. But only a tiny bit.

It's raining. Madison starts to run. There's not far to go now, but when she gets to Luke's house, she's soaking wet anyway.

What's the Matter with Tim?

It feels like forever before anyone hears the doorbell ring.

Madison gets excited when Tim opens the door for her. She wants to say something, maybe about the weather or just hello.

But Tim's eyebrows furrow in what looks like anger, and he says, "Oh, you again."

Madison gasps for air. She barely grabs hold of the front door before it slams shut in her face.

Luke comes down the stairs. "What's with you? Madison has nothing to do with it!" he says to his brother.

Tim yells, "Leave me alone!" and runs up the stairs, shoving Luke aside and slamming his bedroom door behind him.

"What's his problem?" Madison asks.

"It's a bit of a long story," says Luke. "Want some cocoa? And maybe a towel to dry off with?"

Madison accepts both, plus a piece of apple pie. And then Luke tells her what happened.

The Hotrod Derby

"You know how Tim and his friend Andy like to compete in these science fairs? The two of them have always built those great soapbox cars. And how they've come up with a cargo bike? One that's foldable. The thing's also lightweight and looks fun."

"That's so cool!" says Madison.

"Anyway! They really tried their best. They filmed the bike from all sides and showed how to fold it up. Yesterday, they wanted to present it at a big video conference. People from all over the country were logged in," says Luke.

"Actually, they wanted to use the computer at Andy's house. But Andy is totally hoarse with something and also contagious. That's why Tim was going to do it by himself from our house. At two-thirty, it was their turn, and at two, Tim went to set up our laptop. But then he remembered that he still had the flash drive with the videos on it in his jacket. So, he ran down to our coat closet on the first floor and then back up. I think he was pretty nervous by then."

"I would have been, too," says Madison.

Luke continues to tell Madison the story: Then Tim went to get the laptop from Mom's study, but it wasn't there.

"Mom!!" Tim screamed. But Mom isn't there, and the computer isn't either.

"Mom!!" he shouted again, and she came in from the backyard.

"I need the laptop for the presentation!" He was yelling louder and louder now.

"But I thought you were doing it at Andy's house," Mom said.

Tim howled like a wolf.

"It's okay!" Mom told him. "I'll go get it. Since the weather is nice, I figured I'd use it in the yard . . ."

"Run!" Tim shouted.

"Watch your tone," Mom would've normally said, but lucky for him, she bit her tongue.

18

Tim grabbed the laptop and turned it on.

Frantically, he typed the password for his email account. He made a typo three times, but he had to get through. The link to get into the conference was in his email.

Right as the page opened, the laptop ran out of juice.

"Oh," Mom said. "Yep, there was a constant message that the battery would run out soon, but I thought—"

"Whaaat!" Tim screeched. "Where's the charging cord?"

"Uh . . ." Mom said. She looked around wildly. "It was here just now . . ."

"Where?" Tim's voice was barely a squeak.

A Click in the Catastrophe

Luke continued the story. Tim found the charging cord, and Mom put the laptop on Luke's desk since it has significantly more space than Tim's desk.

Then Tim inserted the flash drive with the videos. It was just after two-thirty when he dialed into the conference.

Then he had to get set up. He turned on the camera, the microphone, etc.

"Did I mention that anyone could watch the whole thing live online?" Luke giggled.

"Everyone was waiting for my brother to finally appear on screen. Except the first one to pop up was our cat, Freddy, who absolutely wanted to be in front of the camera. And then Tim, red as a tomato and completely disheveled, popped up."

But this wasn't about Tim himself; it was about the coolest bike in the world. And that's what he wanted to display first with the videos. But they had only tested it at Andy's. And nothing worked on Mom's laptop. Tim almost collapsed. His eyes almost bulged out of his head. He looked like a zombie. But the people were still nice. A girl told him that he had to download a program to make everything work. They selected another group to go first and said he could go right after.

Torooo!

"Phew!" Madison says, relieved. "At least things were working again."

"That's what you think," says Luke. "The worst is yet to come! Guess what kind of project the group—the one that was supposed to go after him—presented."

Madison swallows. "A cargo bike?" she asks, in disbelief.

TOROOO

"Bingo. It wasn't nearly as cool as the one Tim and Andy made. But people just kept yawning throughout Tim's presentation. Andy was so angry and no longer wants to be Tim's friend. And I don't know what annoyed Andy more: that Tim bungled it or that my Benjamin the Elephant poster was on display behind Tim's head the whole time. Totally uncool."

"Torooo!" goes Madison.

Oh Man, How Embarrassing!

"There were a ton of comments about it online. People were splitting ribs from laughing so hard. Tim couldn't be stopped, though, and lashed back with some pretty nasty responses. The worst one was directed at a *flicflac13*. She just wanted to be nice to him and offer some comfort. He insulted her with words I've never read anywhere else. Just awful!" Luke shakes his head.

"Whelp, luckily they didn't use their real names . . . ?" hopes Madison.

"Well, sorta," says Luke. "Flicflac13 knew already that Tim was Soapboxer22."

"Oh, I see. Of course," says Madison.

"And just before you arrived, Tim found out who was hiding behind flicflac13. It's Aileen," Luke continues.

"Tim is totally toast. The day after, he also screwed up his math assignment." Luke snorts. "A full-on catastrophe, for real!"

Madison can't imagine how, after so much fuss, things can ever go back to normal.

Many Thanks, Tim!

On Saturday, Madison is at Luke's, in the backyard. Tim is also there and still bitter, through and through. All of a sudden, Andy appears and shouts over the fence. A company wants to manufacture Andy and Tim's invention and share the profits with them.

When Tim doesn't jump for joy right away, Andy says, "Don't be like that. I would've gotten over it, and we would've made up again, you know."

Tim grins for the first time in too long. It's a little bit off, but at least it's there.

Luke's mom thinks that this is cause to celebrate right away. Madison asks if she can invite another friend and winks at Luke.

In the evening, the lanterns are on, and the smell of barbeque is wonderful. Suddenly, Aileen is standing by the fence. Tim almost chokes on his corn cob.

"Chill out, Soapboxer," she says. "Madison explained the whole mess to me. This time, I forgive you. But only this one time. Understood?"

"Crystal clear, Flicflac," says Tim.

This Is What We'd Like to Know

At school on Monday, Ms. Schwartz says that they are going to participate in a video call like Tim's soon.

"Oh, no," Luke says during recess. "We know everything that can go wrong."

"But that's a good thing!" says Madison. "Because we can prevent it." She takes a notepad and a pen and writes:

Stress-Free Internet: Must-Dos

At Least One Day Ahead of Time:

 I tell everyone in the family when I need to use a device or appliance. This is very important, especially if it's used by several people. We make sure that the device will be free for me to use starting at least one hour before.

 I have already checked out the program that we're going to use to meet. Maybe I need someone to explain how to install or use it.

 We will prearrange where the device and the charging cord will be.

 Do I need anything else? Like a microphone, headset, or earbuds, for example.

 I ask if someone is caring for any pets during the video conference.

 I check the camera beforehand.

 What's in my background when I'm on camera?

 Is it better to look for another place from which to participate?

 Or do I just have to rearrange a little?

 Is the lighting right?

 Is there any ambient sound that I can turn off?

Is everything I might want to show correctly prepared?

 Do I need to do anything else?

 Do I have music to play, pictures, or videos that I can show?

 If I'm using a smartphone or tablet, I might need a stand for it. If I don't have one, I can make one very easily. The main thing is that it be hands-free.

 I could exchange mobile or landline numbers with the other participants. That way we can be reached if something goes wrong with our connection.

gym equipment, preferably!

On the Day of:

 By now, at the latest, I clear up the table where I want to sit. I have only what I need at hand.

 The chair I sit on should not be wobbly.

Up to an Hour Beforehand:

 Am I ready?

 Do I need to eat or drink anything first?

 Or go to the bathroom?

 If I have a mobile phone with me, I silence the ringtone.

 I check again whether the technology is all set.

Half an Hour Beforehand:

 Are the cats and dogs out of the way?

 And the parrot?

 Do the others know that they shouldn't talk or should leave the room by now?

 Do I need to use the bathroom again?

 Do I have everything I need?

Just Before:

 I dial into/connect to the program.

 I wait for a moderator to let me in.

It's Starting:

 We wait until everyone is visible.

 We address one another in greeting.

 We agree on how to get in touch, if we want to tell each other something.

 We then don't talk until the moderator lets us.

 We agree on how long we want to stay on together and when we might take a break.

 When someone else speaks, I listen. I don't talk in between.

While listening, I turn off my own microphone.

 When it's my turn, I turn it on.

 I speak clearly. This is even more important online.

 I don't get up and walk around. That's what the break is for.

 We get each other's attention if something's wrong. For example, when someone's talking and the microphone is still muted.

 We're friendly to each other and don't gripe when someone makes a mistake.

 Finally, we say goodbye properly. Only then do I disconnect from the program.

And in general:

On the Internet, we still deal with each other just as if we'd met "in person." We're even a little friendlier. When chatting online, you can easily be mistaken about something,
which may cause confusion or trouble.

This also applies if someone doesn't write/post using their real name. There's always a real person behind it. Unless it's a troll! But that's another story.
To be safe, we only write to people when we know who they really are.

The first one to read what Madison and Luke have written is Tim.

"Oh man," he says. "That's really cool. You couldn't have done this just a little earlier, though?"

Suggested Reading About Virtual Instruction for Kids

"10 Distance Learning Tips to Help Kids With Virtual School." Children First Canada, posted: January 11, 2021. https://childrenfirstcanada.org /blog/10-distance-learning-tips-to-help-kids-with-virtual-school/

"10 Tips for Navigating Virtual Learning." Strong 4 Life. https://www. strong4life.com/en/schools-and-community/parent-resources/10-tips-for -navigating-virtual-learning

Crowe, Ashley. "10 Virtual Learning Tips for Parents to Support Their Kids in School." Prodigy, posted: September 17, 2021. https://www.prodigyga-me.com/main-en/blog/virtual-learning-tips-for-parents/

Kash, Jeff. "Mastering Focus in Online Training: 3 Techniques for Both You and Your Kids to Acquire and Preserve Concentration." Believing Through Achieving, posted: June 17, 2023. https://btateam.org/mastering -focus-in-online-training-3-techniques-for-both-you-and-your-kids-to-acquire-and-preserve-concentration

Kelin, Alyson. "Virtual Instruction Is Here to Stay. Here Are 7 Tips for Doing It Well." Education Week, posted: April 11, 2022. https://www. edweek.org/technology/virtual-instruction-is-here-to-stay-here-are-7-tips -for-doing-it-well/2022/04

Smith, Sean J. "Distance Learning: 8 Tips to Help Your Child Learn at Home." Understood. https://www.understood.org/en/articles /online-learning-how-to-prepare-child

Srivastava, Surbhi. "11 Amazing Tips to Successfully Prepare Kids for Online Classes." Piggy Ride, posted: October 7, 2020. https://www. piggyride.com/blog/amazing-tips-for-successful-kids-online-classes/

Zaiets, Karina and Janet Loehrke. "These online learning tips will help parents prepare for a successful school year, even if it is virtual." USA Today, posted: August 6, 2020. https://www.usatoday.com/in-depth/ news/2020/08/06/covid-19-tips-parents-successful-online-learning -virtual-classes-zoom/3303918001/

Afterword

Since the coronavirus restricted our contact possibilities, we have realized that there are times when we're happy to be able to meet at least online. When we do this, we are dealing with the pitfalls of technology and have to prepare ourselves differently than when we sit directly opposite each other. This is sometimes not so easy, and things can go wrong, as we can see from Luke's big brother, Tim. So that we can be relaxed and enjoy virtual classes and meetings, it's good to have a checklist. Otherwise, we may still overlook one point or another.

In my story, Madison and Luke have taken on this task and put together a very useful list. When I have my next online meeting, I'll definitely use it.

What also happens is confusion due to user handles, like between Tim and Aileen. Handles are often used on the Internet, and people usually don't know who's behind them. This can be awkward or dangerous. It depends. In any case, it's a topic to be explored in other stories.

Dagmar Geisler

Dagmar Geisler has already supported several generations of parents in accompanying their children through emotionally difficult situations. Through her series Emotional Development for Elementary School Students, the author sensitively deals with the most important issues related to growing up: from body awareness to exploring one's own emotional world to social interactions. Her work always includes a helping of humor. Even when things get serious—then even more so. Her books have been translated into twenty languages and also published in the USA.

Nikolai Renger was born in Karlsruhe and studied visual communication at the HFG in Pforzheim. He works as a freelance illustrator for various publishers and agencies and has been working at Atelier Remise Karlsruhe since 2013.